BRITTLES, BARKS, & BONBONS

DELICIOUS RECIPES for QUICK and EASY CANDY

Charity Ferreira

Photographs by Karen Steffens

CHRONICLE BOOKS

SAN FRANCISCO

Text copyright © 2008 by Charity Ferreira
Photographs copyright © 2008 by Karen Steffens
All rights reserved. No part of this book may be reproduced in
any form without written permission from the publisher.

Library of Congress Cataloging-in-Publication Data available

ISBN: 978-0-8118-5535-8

Manufactured in China

Prop styling by Dianne Mcgauley, Dyan Garza, Alessandra Mortola
Food styling by Robyn Valarik
Designed by Jessica Hische

10 9 8 7 6 5 4 3 2 1

Chronicle Books LLC
680 Second Street
San Francisco, California 94107

www.chroniclebooks.com

Acknowledgments

I am grateful to many people for making this book possible. First, I want to thank my editor and friend Amy Treadwell, and all of the talented people at Chronicle Books. I am also grateful to Sarah Epstein, Marlene Kawahata, Sue Johnson, and Kelly Pfeifer for testing these recipes and giving me invaluable feedback, and to Julie Rolland for fielding all of my questions about French candy. As always, I am deeply indebted to Kate Washington, whose good advice improves everything I do, and to Debbie Hughes, who inspires my best work. Finally, I want to thank my husband, Damon Allswang. In a manner typical of his support for all of my endeavors, he greeted every piece of candy as if it were the best thing he'd ever tasted, and then helped with the dishes afterwards.

For Dylan, Sasha, and Talia,

who are sweeter than all of the candy in this book.

Table of Contents

Introduction

About five years ago, I traveled to Montélimar, France, to write about nougat. The Provençal town is famous for the chewy almond- and pistachio-studded candy, made of egg whites, sugar, and honey, which has a texture somewhere between a Big Hunk bar and the edges of a perfectly staled marshmallow. In town I bought a map, illustrated with little candy icons, that labels the regions of France by the sweets they're known for. I have it on the wall above my desk, and whenever things get hectic I look at it and think about becoming a candy pilgrim, or at least about planning my next vacation around licorice, chocolate-covered cherries, almond paste *calissons*.

One of the best things about being a food writer is being able to pursue what interests and delights me. Whether I'm writing about nougat in Provence, gummy bears in Santa Cruz, saltwater taffy on the Northern California coast, or artisanal chocolate in Berkeley, there's always one wild moment during each interview when I contemplate throwing myself at the feet of the candy maker and begging him or her to take me on as an apprentice. It seems to me that there could be no greater bliss than being surrounded by candy all day, every day.

Candy is so provocative, so transporting. And I don't just mean eating it. I am transported by making it, too. Candy making has a reputation for being difficult, but many kinds of candy are quite simple to make. Caramelizing sugar is a simple process, but it's one of the most magical, transformative things you can do in the kitchen—turning plain white sugar into a crunchy, amber-colored candy with a distinctive, burnt-sugar flavor. Barks and clusters, likewise, are nothing more than melted chocolate with delicious additions like nuts or dried fruit, resulting in a candy that's much greater than the sum of its parts. And the simplest truffles are merely chocolate, cream, and a few flavorings, rolled into bite-size balls and dusted with cocoa powder.

Over the years, I've come to appreciate candy not just for its beauty and flavor, but also for its restraint. Often a bite or two of toffee or a piece of chocolate-dipped fruit is more satisfying than a full-sized dessert. Candy is also an especially unique, personal gift. What could be nicer to receive than a bag of golden sea salt–flavored caramels individually wrapped in squares of waxed paper? Or a few pretty pieces of bark or brittle in a clear cellophane bag tied with a ribbon? How about a box of handmade truffles nestled in paper candy cups?

This book is a collection of the candy I love to make, eat, and share. Many of these are my favorite versions of candy that I've made for years, like the toffees, peanut brittle, and caramels. Others are recipes I developed for specific occasions, holidays, or dinner party menus. Still others are my versions of candy I've come across while traveling in France, like the nougat, the gelées, and the milk chocolate praline. I hope that this book will inspire you to make your own candy, and that some of these recipes will become part of your repertoire.

Ingredients

Chocolate

There are some truly sublime chocolates available today that are well worth the splurge, especially for things like dipping candied orange peel or spreading on top of Buttery Almond Toffee (page 28). However, I admit to a slightly populist leaning when it comes to chocolate, and for most of the recipes in this book—especially ones where the chocolate is flavored with other ingredients—any good, reasonably priced chocolate is a fine choice. I like Callebaut milk chocolate, and I think both Guittard and Ghirardelli make good-tasting, reasonably priced semisweet and bittersweet chocolates. Trader Joe's sells a line of imported Belgian chocolate under its house label that is inexpensive and pleasantly flavorful.

Whether you choose semisweet or bittersweet chocolate is up to you; bittersweet chocolate has a less sweet, more pronounced chocolate flavor. It has become common to see the percentage of cocoa solids noted on the label of dark chocolates. Bittersweet chocolates are usually in the neighborhood of 70 percent cocoa solids, while dark chocolates labeled 50 percent to 60 percent are usually considered semisweet. White chocolate contains no cocoa solids, but check the label to make sure it contains cocoa butter.

Spices, Nuts, and Dried Fruit

Buy spices, nuts, and dried fruit in bulk from somewhere busy, if you can; they are likely to be cheaper and fresher than their prepackaged counterparts. Trader Joe's is a great source for nuts and dried fruit.

Sugar

In 1999, the *San Francisco Chronicle* published a story that rocked the world of every home baker and candy maker who read it. In it, professional baker Carolyn Weil discovered—and the *Chronicle*'s test kitchen confirmed—that cane sugar and beet sugar behave differently in certain applications.

The differences between the two are particularly significant in candy making, where sugar is often the primary ingredient—and where its behavior at high temperatures can make or break your recipe.

In my experience, beet sugar caramelizes less predictably than cane sugar and seems to be more prone to crystallizing.

For these reasons, I always buy C&H granulated sugar. It is the only widely available brand I know of that is specifically labeled "cane sugar." If sugar isn't labeled, it may be either beet sugar or cane sugar. I also like C&H's superfine Baker's Sugar for making candy. The grains are finer than regular granulated sugar, so they dissolve more easily. Baker's sugar is also nice for coating the outside of candies like candied citrus peels or *pâtes de fruits*.

Wrapping and Packaging

You'll be amazed at how much more polished and special homemade candy looks when it's presented in the right packaging—and how easy it is to present your candy beautifully. If you live near a store that sells candy-making supplies, buy yourself a little stock of fluted paper candy cups in various sizes, candy boxes, and clear cellophane treat bags. Or seek out an online source for these items, such as sugarcraft.com. If you have these packaging supplies on hand, you will almost always have the means of making a personal, handmade gift on short notice.

Equipment

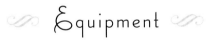

Baking Sheets and Jelly-Roll Pans

Some of the recipes in this book call for a jelly-roll pan—a 10-by-15-inch baking pan with 1-inch-high sides. If the recipe calls for a baking sheet, any cookie sheet will do, either with or without a rim. Baking sheets that are especially battered (I have a few of these in my cabinet) are not the best choices for making brittles and toffees, as the candy tends to stick to places where the finish is scratched, bent, or rusted.

Candy Thermometer

Some of the recipes in this book require a candy thermometer, and you'll find it to be a useful tool for many of the others. Hardware stores and many grocery stores carry them; to make sure you're getting a thermometer that can be used for candy, look for one that measures temperatures up to 400°F.

Chef's Knife

A heavy-duty chef's knife is an indispensable kitchen tool, whether you're making savory food or desserts. If you think you don't cook enough to need a professional-quality knife, I hope you'll reconsider. A good, well-maintained knife is the best way to safely chop chocolate and nuts and to cut candies like caramels and nougat into squares.

Disposable Aluminum Baking Pans

One of the greatest discoveries I made while writing this book is that 8-inch disposable aluminum baking pans, the kind you can buy in packs of three in the baking-supply section of the grocery store, are perfect for making many kinds of candy. Caramels, nougats, gelées—all pop right out when you bend the sides of the pan. I always keep a few of these inexpensive pans on hand.

Flexible Heatproof Spatula

These versatile silicone spatulas can completely cover the bottom surface of a saucepan or bowl, making them the best tool for dissolving sugar in a saucepan, for stirring toffee or caramels, and for stirring chocolate as it gently melts. Most kitchenware and restaurant-supply stores carry them. They aren't cheap, but they are a good investment, as they are fairly indestructible.

Pots and Saucepans

Good-quality, heavy-bottomed cookware is the best choice for cooking sugar mixtures. I like to use a saucepan or pot with a stainless-steel surface so that I can see the color of the sugar as it caramelizes. A 2-quart saucepan that you can lift comfortably with one hand is a good small size; a 3- to 4-quart pan is a good medium size; and a 6-quart pot is a good large size. A good trick for cleaning pots and pans after cooking sticky mixtures like brittles and caramels is to boil a few inches of water in the pot for a minute or two; the sticky candy will dissolve easily in the water.

Candy Tips and Techniques

Caramelizing sugar

Caramelizing sugar for caramels, brittles, and toffees is not difficult, but because the temperatures you're working with are so high, it's wise to be careful. Sugar cooks quickly once it begins to brown, so you'll want to be prepared with everything you'll need to finish the candy. Have all of your ingredients measured and your tools ready before you begin.

Dissolve the sugar completely before bringing the mixture to a boil by stirring it with a flexible spatula over medium-low heat. Many recipes (including some I've written myself) call for washing the sides of the pan down with a clean pastry brush dipped in water to prevent sugar crystals from collecting on the sides of the pan and turning the entire mixture into a grainy mess. At some point in my years of candy making, I started skipping this step, and I haven't crystallized a pan of sugar yet. Dissolving the sugar completely before you bring the mixture to a boil is your best defense against crystallization. You can also run the spatula around the inside of the pan a few times as the sugar is dissolving to remove any visible clumps of sugar from the sides of the pan.

Once the sugar begins to brown, if it looks like the mixture is getting dark around the edges of the pan but is still clear in the center, you can lift the pan carefully and gently swirl the mixture a few times to help it caramelize more evenly.

Melting Chocolate

If you've worked much with chocolate, you probably know that chocolate falls out of "temper" when melted. In a bar of chocolate straight from the manufacturer, the cocoa butter and chocolate solids are suspended in a delicate balance that makes the chocolate bar shiny and hard. Melting the chocolate disrupts this delicate suspension, and when the chocolate cools it can be tacky to the touch or have dull gray streaks on the surface.

To be perfectly honest, even though I work with chocolate all the time, I almost never temper my chocolate. It's a multistep process involving several different precise temperatures, and it's difficult to do with small amounts of chocolate. When I make barks, clusters, or chocolate-dipped candy, I do two things to make sure the chocolate sets up nicely.

First, I use a modified version of the "direct method" of tempering that I read about in *Chocolatier* magazine several years ago. This method entails melting the chocolate so gently that it never gets hotter than 91°F, and thus never falls out of temper in the first place. Chop the chocolate very finely; the more finely it is chopped, the more quickly and evenly it will melt. Place the chocolate in a metal or glass bowl that will fit on top of a pan filled with a few inches of water (the bottom of the bowl should not touch the water). Bring the water to a simmer, turn off the heat, and then place the bowl of chocolate over the hot water. Stir the chocolate frequently with a flexible spatula to encourage even melting. If you need to, you can remove the bowl, reheat the water, and replace the bowl. Once the chocolate is melted, remove the bowl from the pan, stir it well, and use it immediately. This slow, gentle melting is most important for milk chocolate and white chocolate, which will clump and refuse to melt smoothly if they get too hot.

Second, if I plan to hold on to the chocolate-dipped candy longer than a day or two, I treat it as a perishable item and store it in the refrigerator, removing it to serve or eat. This may be counter to everything you've heard before about storing chocolate, but it keeps the chocolate firm and fresh. Once removed from the refrigerator, the chocolate's surface will dull after a few days, but it's pretty rare that anything that's been dipped in chocolate hangs around my house long enough for that to happen.

Toasting Nuts

Toasting nuts brings out their flavor and makes them taste crisp and fresh. To toast nuts, bake them at 350°F in a shallow baking pan or on a baking sheet, just until fragrant and golden, 5 to 10 minutes.

Using a Candy Thermometer

Attach the candy thermometer (most of them have a built-in clip) to the side of the pan after the sugar mixture has come to a boil. To measure the temperature of the sugar mixture accurately, the heat sensor must be completely submerged. Some thermometers have a mark indicating where the sensor is; most models need to be submerged at least an inch deep. If the sugar mixture is not deep enough, you can carefully tilt the pan to check the temperature

You can test the accuracy of your candy thermometer by submerging it in boiling water (it should read 212°F). For many of the recipes in this book, however, your best doneness test is a visual one: when in doubt, go by the color of the sugar mixture.

Brittles and Toffees

Whether you're a loyal fan of classics like almond toffee or peanut brittle or want to try something a little different, like rich, crunchy Pine Nut Honeycomb (page 27), you will find something irresistible in this chapter. Because brittles and toffees keep well, they are particularly good choices for gift giving. Large, shiny, irregularly shaped pieces are beautiful tucked into a clear cellophane bag and tied with a ribbon. Or, you can break the candy into smaller chunks and place each piece into a little paper candy cup, which you can arrange on a plate or in a gift box.

Brittles and toffees are also great for adding a pastry chef's touch to your favorite desserts. Sprinkle a handful of Coconut-Peanut Toffee (page 23) pieces over a scoop of coconut ice cream, prop a few shards of Spicy Pepita Brittle (page 20) on top of a pumpkin-flavored custard, or end a Spanish paella party with sherry-soaked butter cake garnished with a few pieces of Spanish Almond Brittle (page 17).

Old-Fashioned Peanut Brittle

This recipe is adapted from Jean van Stein's recipe for peanut brittle. Chef Jean was one of my instructors at the California Culinary Academy in San Francisco. She said her grandmother's recipe made the best peanut brittle, and she was right! ✍ Makes: 1 ½ pounds brittle

¼ cup (½ stick) unsalted butter, cut into chunks, plus more for pan

1 teaspoon baking soda

¼ teaspoon salt

1 tablespoon vanilla extract

2 ½ cups sugar

½ cup water

⅓ cup light corn syrup

2 cups roasted, unsalted peanuts (about 10 ounces)

Step 1	Lightly butter a 10-by-15-inch jelly-roll pan. Dissolve the baking soda and salt in the vanilla extract and set aside.
Step 2	In a large pot over medium heat, stir together the sugar, water, corn syrup, and ¼ cup butter until the sugar is dissolved and the butter is melted. Increase the heat and boil, stirring occasionally with a heatproof spatula or a wooden spoon, until the mixture turns a deep golden brown and measures 335° to 340°F on a candy thermometer, 10 to 15 minutes. Remove from the heat and carefully (the mixture will bubble up) stir in the vanilla mixture and peanuts.
Step 3	Immediately pour into the prepared pan. If necessary, use a spatula or wooden spoon to spread the mixture flat. Let stand at room temperature until cool and hard, about 1 hour.
Step 4	Bend the ends of the pan to release the brittle (run a spatula underneath the brittle to help release it, if necessary) and chop or break into chunks. Store in an airtight container in the refrigerator for up to 2 weeks.

Spanish Almond Brittle

This sophisticated brittle is the brainchild of food writer Kate Washington. It is delicious on its own, but it's also a lovely addition to a fruit and cheese plate. Spanish smoked paprika (*pimentón*) has a wonderful, subtly smoky flavor. Look for it at stores that sell imported Spanish foods, or at spanishtable.com. Makes: 2 pounds brittle

Note

Measure the nuts, paprika, and salt before you start, so that they're ready to stir in the moment the sugar reaches the desired amber color.

Butter, for pan

2 teaspoons sweet smoked paprika (*pimentón dulce*)

¼ teaspoon salt

3 cups sugar

1 cup water

2 tablespoons light corn syrup

2 cups blanched slivered almonds (about 12 ounces), lightly toasted

Step 1

Lightly butter a 10-by-15-inch jelly-roll pan. In a small bowl, stir together the paprika and salt; set aside.

Continued on page 19

[Spanish Almond Brittle]

Step 2   In a medium saucepan over medium-low heat, stir together the sugar, water, and corn syrup until the sugar is completely dissolved, about 5 minutes. Increase the heat to high and boil without stirring until the syrup is golden brown (about 335°F on a candy thermometer), 5 to 10 minutes. When the sugar begins to brown around the edges of the pan, swirl the pan gently so that it caramelizes evenly.

Step 3   Remove from the heat and carefully (the mixture will bubble up) stir in the nuts and paprika mixture. Immediately pour into the prepared pan. Let stand at room temperature until cool and hard, about 1 hour.

Step 4   Bend the ends of the pan to release the brittle (run a spatula underneath the brittle to help release it, if necessary) and chop or break into chunks. Store at room temperature in an airtight container for up to 2 weeks.

Spicy Pepita Brittle

This is a beautiful, unusual brittle. If you like things very spicy, increase the cayenne to 2 teaspoons. Measure out the pepitas, cayenne, and salt before you start, so that they're ready to stir in the moment the sugar reaches the desired amber color. *Makes: 2 pounds brittle*

Butter, for pan

1 ½ teaspoons cayenne pepper

¼ teaspoon salt

3 cups sugar

1 cup water

2 tablespoons light corn syrup

2 cups pepitas (hulled pumpkin seeds; about 8 ounces), lightly toasted

Step 1 — **Lightly butter** a 10-by-15-inch jelly-roll pan. In a small bowl, stir together the cayenne and salt; set aside.

Step 2 — **In a medium saucepan** over medium heat, stir together the sugar, water, and corn syrup until the sugar is completely dissolved, about 5 minutes. Increase the heat to high and boil without stirring until the syrup is golden brown (about 335°F on a candy thermometer), 10 to 15 minutes. When the sugar begins to brown around the edges of the pan, swirl the pan gently so that it caramelizes evenly. Remove from the heat and carefully (the mixture will bubble and the pepitas may "pop") stir in the pepitas and cayenne mixture.

Step 3 — **Immediately pour** into the prepared pan, using a spatula or wooden spoon to spread the nuts out flat if necessary. Let the brittle stand at room temperature until cool and hard, about 1 hour.

Step 4 — **Bend the ends** of the pan to release the brittle (run a spatula underneath the brittle to help release it, if necessary) and chop or break into chunks. Store in an airtight container at room temperature for up to 2 weeks.

Coconut-Peanut Toffee

This is one of the candies I can't stop eating; the peanuts and coconut are delicious with the buttery flavor of the toffee. With some sliced mango, it would make a great dessert after a Southeast Asian meal. You'll find unsweetened coconut at natural foods stores and international markets. ∞ Makes: 2 pounds toffee

1 ¼ cups (2 ½ sticks) unsalted butter, cut into chunks, plus more for pan

3 ⅓ cups sugar

¾ cup water

¼ cup light corn syrup

½ teaspoon salt

1 cup toasted unsalted peanuts (about 5 ounces), finely chopped

½ cup unsweetened, dried coconut

2 teaspoons vanilla extract

Step 1	Lightly butter a 10-by-15-inch jelly-roll pan.
Step 2	In a large pot over medium-low heat, stir together the sugar, 1¼ cups butter, the water, corn syrup, and salt until the sugar is dissolved and the butter is melted. Increase the heat until the mixture is simmering and cook, stirring occasionally with a heatproof spatula or wooden spoon, until the mixture turns a deep golden brown and measures 290° to 300°F on a candy thermometer, 10 to 15 minutes. Remove from the heat and carefully (the mixture will bubble up) stir in the peanuts, coconut, and vanilla.
Step 3	Immediately pour into the prepared pan. If necessary, use a heatproof spatula or wooden spoon to spread the mixture flat. Let stand at room temperature until cool and hard, about 1 hour.
Step 4	Bend the ends of the pan to release the toffee (run a spatula underneath the toffee to help release it, if necessary) and chop or break into chunks. Store in an airtight container in the refrigerator for up to 2 weeks.

✎ Macadamia Nut Brittle ✎

Rich, golden, and studded with buttery macadamia nuts, this candy transcends all other brittles. ✎ Makes: 2 pounds brittle

6 tablespoons (¾ stick) unsalted butter, cut into chunks, plus more for pan

½ teaspoon baking soda

1 tablespoon vanilla extract

2 ½ cups sugar

½ cup water

⅓ cup light corn syrup

¼ teaspoon salt

2 cups macadamia nuts (about 12 ounces), lightly toasted and roughly chopped

Step 1 — **Lightly butter** a 10-by-15-inch jelly-roll pan. Dissolve the baking soda in the vanilla extract; set aside.

Step 2 — **In a large pot** over medium-low heat, stir together the sugar, water, 6 tablespoons butter, the corn syrup, and salt until the sugar is dissolved and the butter is melted. Increase the heat and cook, stirring occasionally with a heatproof spatula or wooden spoon, until the mixture turns a deep golden brown and measures about 335°F on a candy thermometer, 10 to 15 minutes. Remove from the heat and carefully (the mixture will bubble up) stir in the vanilla mixture and nuts.

Step 3 — **Immediately pour** into the prepared pan. If necessary, use a spatula or wooden spoon to spread the mixture flat. Let stand at room temperature until cool and hard, about 1 hour.

Step 4 — **Bend the ends** of the pan to release the brittle (run a spatula underneath the brittle to help release it, if necessary) and chop or break into chunks. Store in an airtight container in the refrigerator for up to 2 weeks.

Pine Nut Honeycomb

With its honey overtones and the subtle, resiny flavor of the pine nuts, this brittle-like candy is delicious after a meal with Greek or Mediterranean flavors. The baking soda gives it a porous, crunchy texture. *Makes: 1 pound brittle*

¼ cup (½ stick) unsalted butter, cut in chunks, plus more for pan

1 teaspoon baking soda

1 ½ teaspoons vanilla extract

½ cup water

2 ½ cups sugar

⅓ cup honey

¼ teaspoon salt

1½ cups pine nuts (about 6 ounces), lightly toasted

Step 1   **Lightly butter** a 10-by-15-inch jelly-roll pan. In a small bowl, dissolve the baking soda in the vanilla; set aside.

Step 2   **In a large pot** over medium-low heat, stir together the sugar, water, honey, ¼ cup butter, and the salt until the sugar is dissolved and the butter is melted. Increase the heat and cook, stirring occasionally with a heatproof spatula or wooden spoon, until the mixture turns a deep golden brown and measures about 300°F on a candy thermometer, 8 to 12 minutes. Remove from the heat and carefully (the mixture will bubble up) stir in the vanilla mixture and pine nuts.

Step 3   **Immediately pour** into the prepared pan. Let stand at room temperature until cool and hard, about 30 minutes.

Step 4   **Bend the ends** of the pan to release the brittle (run a spatula underneath the brittle to help release it, if necessary) and chop or break into chunks. Store in an airtight container in the refrigerator for up to 2 weeks.

❧ Buttery Almond Toffee ❧

The flavors of sweet butter, caramelized sugar, toasted almonds, and dark chocolate are beautifully balanced in this classic English toffee. ❧ Makes: 3 pounds toffee

1½ cups (3 sticks) unsalted butter, cut into chunks, plus more for pan

3½ cups sugar

¾ cup water

¼ cup light corn syrup

½ teaspoon salt

2 teaspoons vanilla extract

1½ cups whole almonds (about 9 ounces), toasted and chopped

12 ounces bittersweet or semisweet chocolate, chopped

Step 1   Lightly butter a 10-by-15-inch jelly-roll pan.

Step 2   In a large pot over medium heat, stir together the sugar, 1½ cups butter, water, corn syrup, and salt until the sugar is dissolved and the butter is melted and bubbling. Increase the heat and boil, stirring occasionally with a wooden spoon or a heatproof spatula, until the mixture turns a deep golden brown and measures 290° to 300°F on a candy thermometer, 10 to 15 minutes. Remove from the heat and carefully (the mixture will bubble up) stir in half of the almonds and the vanilla.

Continued on page 30

[Buttery Almond Toffee]

Step 3 **Immediately pour** into the prepared pan. If necessary, use a spatula or wooden spoon to spread the mixture flat. Let stand at room temperature until cool and hard, about 45 minutes.

Step 4 **While the toffee cools,** melt the chocolate in a bowl set over a pan of hot water (see Melting Chocolate, page 12), stirring frequently until melted and smooth. Remove from the heat.

Step 5 **Pour the chocolate** over the cooled toffee, spreading it to the edges with a knife or spatula. Sprinkle the remaining almonds over the chocolate. Refrigerate to set the chocolate, about 30 minutes.

Step 6 **Bend the ends** of the pan to release the toffee and chop or break into chunks. Store in an airtight container in the refrigerator for up to 2 weeks.

∽ Cinnamon Brittle ∽

Debbie Hughes, the pastry chef at Firefly in San Francisco, invented this combination of spicy cinnamon and caramelized sugar, which reminds me of a gourmet version of Red Hots candies. ∽ *Makes:* 1 pound brittle

¼ cup (½ stick) unsalted butter, plus more for pan

1 teaspoon baking soda

1 teaspoon vanilla extract

1 tablespoon ground cinnamon

½ teaspoon salt

2 ½ cups sugar

½ cup water

⅓ cup light corn syrup

Step 1	**Lightly butter** a 10-by-15-inch jelly-roll pan. In a small bowl or measuring cup, dissolve the baking soda in the vanilla extract and set aside. In another bowl, stir together the cinnamon and salt (this will make the cinnamon easier to distribute when you stir it into the sugar mixture).
Step 2	**In a large pot** over medium-low heat, stir together the sugar, water, corn syrup, and ¼ cup butter until the sugar is dissolved and the butter is melted. Increase the heat and cook, stirring occasionally with a heatproof spatula or a wooden spoon, until the mixture turns a deep golden brown and measures 335° to 340°F on a candy thermometer, 8 to 12 minutes. Remove from the heat and carefully (the mixture will bubble up) stir in the vanilla and cinnamon mixtures.
Step 3	**Immediately pour** into the prepared pan. Let stand at room temperature until cool and hard, about 30 minutes.
Step 4	**Bend the ends** of the pan to release the brittle (run a spatula underneath the brittle to help release it, if necessary) and chop or break into chunks. Store in an airtight container in the refrigerator for up to 2 weeks.

Barks and Clusters

There must be some archetypal reason that chocolate with chunks is so appealing. When I was making the barks for this chapter, I loved each combination more than the last, and I realized that there's really no end to the possibilities. Barks can be sophiticated, like Dark Chocolate Bark with Figs, Almonds, and Anise (page 34), or whimsical, like Peanut-Raisin Bark (page 39). I think of clusters as sort of the inverse of barks—more chunks, less chocolate. Both barks and clusters lend themselves well to improvising, so feel free to customize them with your own favorite ingredients. These are some of the quickest and easiest candies to make, which means they're great choices for homemade gifts in the busy holiday season, snacks for movie night, or sweet nibbles to have around the house.

Dark Chocolate Bark with Figs, Almonds, and Anise

This is a dark, fruity bark for sophisticated chocolate lovers. A plate piled high with jagged shards makes a great casual dessert with coffee after an Italian meal. ✍ Makes: 1 ½ pounds bark

1 pound bittersweet chocolate, chopped

1½ cups whole almonds (about 9 ounces), toasted

1 cup chopped dried black Mission figs

2 teaspoons whole anise seeds

Step 1 — **Line a jelly-roll pan** with waxed paper. Melt the chocolate in a bowl set over a pan of hot water (see Melting Chocolate, page 12), stirring frequently until melted and smooth. Remove from the heat.

Step 2 — **Stir in 1 cup** of the almonds and the figs and anise. Scrape the mixture onto the pan and spread out with a spatula to about ½ inch thick. Sprinkle the remaining almonds over the top, gently pressing them into the chocolate to adhere.

Step 3 — **Refrigerate the bark** until completely firm, about 2 hours. Break or cut into chunks. Store in an airtight container at room temperature for up to 1 day, or in the refrigerator for up to 2 weeks.

Chocolate-Cherry-Hazelnut Bark

Dark chocolate, tart cherries, and toasted hazelnuts evoke the flavors of the Pacific Northwest. You can slough off some of the toasted hazelnut skin if you want to, but don't worry about it otherwise. Once it's covered in dark chocolate you won't notice the difference. Makes: 1 ½ pounds bark

1 pound bittersweet chocolate, chopped

¾ cup hazelnuts (about 4 ounces), toasted

½ cup dried tart cherries

Step 1   **Line a jelly-roll pan** with waxed paper. Melt the chocolate in a bowl set over a pan of hot water (see Melting Chocolate, page 12), stirring frequently until melted and smooth. Remove from the heat.

Step 2   **Stir in the hazelnuts** and cherries. Scrape the mixture onto the pan and spread out with a spatula to ¼-to ½-inch thick.

Step 3   **Refrigerate the bark** until completely firm, about 2 hours. Break or cut into chunks. Store in an airtight container at room temperature for up to 1 day, or in the refrigerator for up to 2 weeks.

Rocky Road Bark

It doesn't get much simpler, or more delicious, than this old-fashioned combination.
Makes: 1 ½ pounds bark

1 pound bittersweet chocolate, chopped

2 cups miniature marshmallows

1 ½ cups pecan pieces (about 8 ounces), lightly toasted

Step 1   **Line a jelly-roll pan** with waxed paper. Melt the chocolate in a bowl set over a pan of hot water (see Melting Chocolate, page 12), stirring frequently until melted and smooth. Remove from the heat.

Step 2   **Stir in 1 ½ cups** of the marshmallows and 1 cup of the pecans. Scrape the mixture onto the pan and spread out with a spatula to ½ inch thick. Sprinkle the remaining marshmallows and pecans over the top, gently pressing them into the chocolate to adhere.

Step 3   **Refrigerate the bark** until completely firm, about 2 hours. Break or cut into chunks. Store in an airtight container at room temperature for up to 1 day, or in the refrigerator for up to 2 weeks.

Crispy Rice Bark

This bark is like a giant, homemade Nestlé Crunch bar. ∞ Makes: 1 pound bark

1 pound milk chocolate, chopped
1 ¼ cups Rice Krispies or other puffed rice cereal

Step 1   **Line a jelly-roll pan** with waxed paper. Melt the chocolate in a bowl set over a pan of hot water (see Melting Chocolate, page 12), stirring frequently until melted and smooth. Remove from the heat.

Step 2   **Stir in the cereal.** Scrape the mixture onto the pan and spread out with a spatula to ¼ to ½ inch thick.

Step 3   **Refrigerate the bark** until completely firm, about 2 hours. Break or cut into chunks. Store in an airtight container at room temperature for up to 1 day, or in the refrigerator for up to 2 weeks.

Peanut-Raisin Bark

I thought about calling this "movie bark," because it puts Goobers and Raisinets to shame. Make it for someone you love and pass it to them in the dark at the movies. ✍ Makes: 1½ pounds bark

1 pound milk chocolate, chopped
2 cups unsalted peanuts (about 12 ounces), toasted
1½ cups raisins

Step 1   Line a jelly-roll pan with waxed paper. Melt the chocolate in a bowl set over a pan of hot water (see Melting Chocolate, page 12), stirring frequently until melted and smooth. Remove from the heat.

Step 2   Stir in the peanuts and raisins. Scrape the mixture onto the pan and spread out with a spatula to about ½-inch thick.

Step 3   Refrigerate the bark until firm, about 2 hours. Break or cut into chunks. Store in an airtight container at room temperature for up to 1 day, or in the refrigerator for up to 2 weeks.

Marbled Peppermint Bark

This bark is equally lovely as a dessert or gift around the holidays. Miniature candy canes, the ones that come individually wrapped, work best for this recipe. They are easier to crush, and, because they have more colored surface area, they break into nicer-looking pieces than larger candy canes. If you are a perfectionist, you can sift the candy cane pieces through a fine mesh strainer to remove the fine white dust before sprinkling them over the top of the bark.

Makes: 1¼ pounds bark

1 pound bittersweet or semisweet chocolate, chopped
4 ounces white chocolate, chopped
1 cup finely crushed candy cane pieces

Step 1
Line a jelly-roll pan with waxed paper. Melt the chocolate in a bowl set over a pan of hot water (see Melting Chocolate, page 12), stirring frequently until melted and smooth. Remove from the heat.

Step 2
In another bowl, melt the white chocolate as above.

Step 3
Stir ¾ cup of the candy cane pieces into the dark chocolate. Scrape the mixture onto the pan and spread out with a spatula to about ¼ inch thick. Drizzle the white chocolate evenly over the dark chocolate; use a knife to gently swirl the dark and white chocolates together, leaving plenty of distinct streaks. Sprinkle the remaining crushed candy canes evenly over the top.

Step 4
Refrigerate the bark until completely firm, about 2 hours. Break or cut into chunks. Store in an airtight container at room temperature for up to 1 day, or in the refrigerator for up to 2 weeks.

Sea Turtles

Made with salted caramels and tropical cashews for the "flippers," these clusters are a whimsical varation on a classic candy. This is a great way to use up any irregular trimmings from the Vanilla–Sea Salt Caramels (page 74). Or feel free to use purchased soft caramels—Kraft caramels work fine, although they won't have the same salty edge. The turtles will taste best if you give them a few minutes at room temperature before eating. *Makes: about 24 turtles*

Butter, for waxed paper

8 ounces Vanilla–Sea Salt Caramels (page 74) or store-bought soft caramels (about 24 caramels or 1 ¼ cups)

1 ¼ cups unsalted whole cashews (about 5 ounces), lightly toasted

4 ounces bittersweet or semisweet chocolate, chopped

Step 1 — **Line a baking sheet** with generously buttered waxed paper. Unwrap the caramels and place them in a large heatproof bowl over a pan of barely simmering water. Stir the caramels occasionally until melted and smooth, 10 to 20 minutes. Remove from the heat and stir in the cashews.

Step 2 — **Spoon 1-inch mounds** of the caramel mixture onto the waxed paper. If the mixture is stiff, you might have to use your fingers to coax it into clusters. Refrigerate the clusters until the caramel is firm, about 15 minutes.

Step 3 — **Melt the chocolate** in a bowl set over a pan of hot water (see Melting Chocolate, page 12), stirring frequently until melted and smooth. Remove from the heat.

Step 4 — **Spoon about 1 teaspoon** melted chocolate over the top of each "turtle." Return the "turtles" to the refrigerator to harden the chocolate, about 1 hour. Store in an airtight container in the refrigerator for up to 2 weeks.

White Chocolate Clusters with Pistachios and Golden Raisins

Multicolored, candied fennel seeds give color and a unique flavor to these clusters. Look for them in Indian or international markets. ✍ **Makes:** about 24 clusters

8 ounces white chocolate, chopped

¾ cup shelled pistachio nuts (about 3 ounces), lightly toasted

⅓ cup golden raisins

1 ½ tablespoons candied fennel seeds

Step 1 **Line a baking sheet** with waxed paper. Melt the chocolate in a bowl set over a pan of hot water (see Melting Chocolate, page 12), stirring frequently until melted and smooth. Remove from the heat and stir in the nuts and raisins.

Step 2 **Spoon tablespoon-size mounds** of the mixture onto the waxed paper. Sprinkle the tops with the fennel seeds. Refrigerate until the clusters are firm, about 1 hour. Store in an airtight container in the refrigerator for up to 2 weeks.

Coconut-Smoked Almond Haystacks

The smoked almonds give these chocolate clusters a mysterious, appealing edge. If you prefer, you can substitute plain toasted almonds. *Makes: 16 to 18 clusters*

8 ounces bittersweet or semisweet chocolate, chopped

1 ½ cups sweetened flaked coconut

¾ cup smoked almonds (about 5 ounces), finely chopped

Step 1   **Line a baking sheet** with waxed paper. Melt the chocolate in a large heatproof bowl over a pan of hot water (see Melting Chocolate, page 12), stirring frequently until melted and smooth. Remove from the heat.

Step 2   **Stir in 1 cup of the coconut** and ½ cup of the almonds. Spoon the mixture in heaping tablespoon-size mounds onto the waxed paper. Mix the remaining coconut and almonds in a bowl and sprinkle them over the tops of the haystacks, lightly pressing them into the chocolate to adhere.

Step 3   **Refrigerate until firm,** about 1 hour. Store in an airtight container at room temperature for up to 1 day, or in the refrigerator for up to 2 weeks.

Chocolate Pretzel Clusters

Both milk chocolate and white chocolate are delicious with the salty, biscuitlike crunch of the pretzels in these clusters, so use whichever you like better. Or make some of each. These are a fun TV-watching snack, and they also make a great ice-cream topping. Makes: about 30 clusters

8 ounces milk or white chocolate, chopped

2 cups miniature salted pretzels

Step 1   **Line a baking sheet** with waxed paper. Melt the chocolate in a bowl set over a pan of hot water (see Melting Chocolate, page 12), stirring frequently until melted and smooth. Remove from the heat and stir in the pretzels.

Step 2   **Use a spoon to drop clusters** of 2 or 3 pretzels onto the waxed paper. Refrigerate until the chocolate is firm, about 1 hour. Store in an airtight container in the refrigerator for up to 2 weeks.

Truffles and Chocolate-Dipped Candies

These are the sweets that make me feel like a chocolatier, stirring subtle aromatics into already complex and character-filled dark chocolate for truffles, or transforming unassuming snacks like graham crackers, or dried fruit into spectacular gourmet treats by dipping them in chocolate. As simple as they are, the candies in this chapter have a remarkable impact. A chocolate-dipped strawberry after a light spring meal, a chocolate-covered graham cracker with a glass of cold milk, or a bite-size truffle and a cup of after-dinner coffee—these are treats to savor.

Malted Milk Chocolate Truffles

Malted milk powder is essentially a nutritional supplement, but it has a sweet, toasty milk flavor (think malt balls and malted milkshakes) that makes it a popular partner for chocolate. Look for it near the cocoa in the grocery store. For the best flavor, bring these truffles to room temperature before eating. ✤ Makes: about 36 (¾-inch) truffles

8 ounces bittersweet chocolate, chopped

4 ounces milk chocolate, chopped

½ cup malted milk powder

¾ cup whipping cream

2 tablespoons powdered sugar

2 tablespoons unsweetened cocoa powder

Fluted 1-inch paper candy cups (optional)

Step 1
Place the chocolates in a large bowl. In a small saucepan, stir the malted milk powder into the cream and bring to a boil. Pour the cream mixture over the chocolate and stir gently with a flexible spatula until the chocolate is melted and smooth. (If the chocolate does not melt completely, place the bowl over a pan of hot water and stir until smooth.) Cover with plastic wrap and refrigerate until firm enough to scoop, about 3 hours.

Step 2
Line a baking sheet with waxed paper. Scoop out tablespoon-size portions of the chocolate mixture; place them on the waxed paper. If the mixture is too firm to scoop, let it stand at room temperature for about 30 minutes to soften.

Step 3
Partially mix the powdered sugar and cocoa on a plate, so that the colors are marbled. Dust your hands lightly with the mixture. Shape each scoop into a ball, then roll it in the cocoa mixture to coat. Place each truffle in a paper candy cup, if desired. Refrigerate the truffles between layers of waxed paper in an airtight container for up to 1 week.

Chocolate-Sour Cream Truffles

Tangy sour cream enhances the flavor of the dark chocolate in these truffles. For the best flavor, bring them to room temperature before eating. ✖ Makes: 25 to 30 (¾-inch) truffles

10 ounces bittersweet chocolate, finely chopped

2 ounces unsweetened chocolate, finely chopped

¼ cup packed brown sugar

1 tablespoon unsalted butter

¾ cup sour cream

⅓ cup unsweetened cocoa powder

Fluted 1-inch paper candy cups (optional)

Step 1 **In a bowl set over a pan** of barely simmering water, stir together the chocolates, brown sugar, and butter until melted and smooth. Remove from the heat and stir in the sour cream until well blended. Cover with plastic wrap and refrigerate until firm enough to scoop, about 2 hours.

Step 2 **Line a baking sheet** with waxed paper. Scoop out tablespoon-size portions of the chocolate mixture; place them on the waxed paper. If the mixture is too firm to scoop, let it stand at room temperature for about 30 minutes to soften.

Step 3 **Spread the cocoa on a plate.** Dust your hands lightly with cocoa. Shape each scoop into a ball and roll it in cocoa to coat. Place each truffle in a paper candy cup, if desired. Refrigerate the truffles between layers of waxed paper in an airtight container for up to 1 week.

Chai-Spiced Truffles

The fragrant spices that flavor Indian black tea—cinnamon, clove, and cardamom—are also a delicious complement to dark chocolate. For the best flavor, bring the truffles to room temperature before eating. ∞ Makes: about 24 (¾-inch) truffles

12 ounces bittersweet or semisweet chocolate, finely chopped

¾ cup whipping cream

1 tablespoon vanilla extract

3 tablespoons unsweetened cocoa powder

1 teaspoon ground cinnamon

½ teaspoon ground cardamom

¼ teaspoon ground cloves

Fluted 1-inch paper candy cups (optional)

Step 1 **Place the chopped chocolate** in a large bowl. In a small saucepan, bring the cream to a boil. Pour the cream over the chocolate and stir gently with a flexible spatula until the chocolate is melted and smooth. (If the chocolate does not melt completely, place the bowl over a pan of hot water and stir until smooth.) Stir in the vanilla. Cover with plastic wrap and refrigerate until firm enough to scoop, at least 3 hours.

Step 2 **Line a baking sheet** with waxed paper. Scoop out tablespoon-size portions of the chocolate mixture; place them on the waxed paper. If the mixture is too firm to scoop, let it stand at room temperature for about 30 minutes to soften.

Step 3 **Stir together the cocoa** and spices on a plate. Dust your hands lightly with the cocoa mixture. Shape each scoop into a ball, then roll it in the cocoa mixture to coat. Place the truffles in paper cups, if desired. Refrigerate the truffles between layers of waxed paper in an airtight container for up to 1 week.

Mexican Chocolate Truffles

Adding chile to chocolate is not as trendy an idea as it might seem. The Aztecs flavored their chocolate with a variety of spices—including chiles—that enhance the complex flavors already present in dark chocolate. If you want just a hint of spice in these truffles, use ⅛ teaspoon cayenne; if you want to really taste the heat, use ¼ teaspoon. Makes: 30 (¾-inch) truffles

12 ounces semisweet chocolate, chopped

¾ cup whipping cream

2 tablespoons Kahlúa

½ teaspoon almond extract

½ teaspoon plus 1 tablespoon ground cinnamon

⅛ to ¼ teaspoon cayenne pepper

¼ cup unsweetened cocoa powder

Fluted 1-inch paper candy cups (optional)

Step 1   **Place the chocolate** in a large bowl. In a small saucepan, bring the cream to a boil. Pour the cream over the chocolate and stir gently with a flexible spatula until the chocolate is melted and smooth. (If the chocolate does not melt completely, place the bowl over a pan of hot water and stir until smooth.) Stir in the Kahlúa, almond extract, ½ teaspoon of the cinnamon, and the cayenne. Cover with plastic wrap and refrigerate until firm enough to scoop, about 3 hours.

Continued on page 58

[Mexican Chocolate Truffles]

Step 2   **Line a baking sheet** with waxed paper. Scoop out tablespoon-size portions of the chocolate mixture; place them on the waxed paper. If the mixture is too firm to scoop, let it stand at room temperature for about 30 minutes to soften.

Step 3   **Stir together the cocoa** and the remaining 1 tablespoon of cinnamon on a plate. Dust your hands lightly with the cocoa mixture. Shape each scoop into a ball, then roll it in the cocoa mixture to coat. Place each truffle in a paper candy cup, if desired. Refrigerate the truffles between layers of waxed paper in an airtight container for up to 1 week.

Dark Chocolate–Espresso Truffles

These truffles are the perfect bite of something sweet with an after-dinner cup of coffee. For the best flavor, bring them to room temperature before eating. ∞ Makes: 24 (¾-inch) truffles

12 ounces bittersweet chocolate, finely chopped

1½ tablespoons instant espresso powder

¾ cup whipping cream

1 tablespoon Kahlúa

¼ cup unsweetened cocoa powder

Fluted 1-inch paper candy cups (optional)

Step 1   **Place the chopped chocolate** in a large bowl. In a small saucepan over medium heat, dissolve the espresso powder in the cream and bring to a boil. Pour the cream mixture over the chocolate and stir gently with a flexible spatula until the chocolate is melted and smooth. (If the chocolate does not melt completely, place the bowl over a pan of hot water and stir until smooth.) Stir in the Kahlúa. Cover with plastic wrap and refrigerate until firm enough to scoop, at least 3 hours.

Step 2   **Line a baking sheet** with waxed paper. Scoop out tablespoon-size portions of the chocolate mixture; place them on the waxed paper. If the mixture is too firm to scoop, let it stand at room temperature for about 30 minutes to soften.

Step 3   **Spread the cocoa on a plate.** Dust your hands lightly with cocoa. Shape each scoop of the chocolate mixture into a ball, then roll it in the cocoa to coat. Place the truffles in paper candy cups, if desired. Refrigerate the truffles between sheets of waxed paper in an airtight container for up to 1 week.

Mocha-Hazelnut Truffles

Espresso and Frangelico flavor these creamy white chocolate truffles. I like them with an afternoon cappuccino (although sometimes I skip the cappuccino). To skin the hazelnuts, bake them in a 350°F oven until golden brown under their papery skins, 10 to 12 minutes. Let the nuts cool and then rub them vigorously in a clean kitchen towel to remove the loose skins. ∞ Makes: 36 (¾-inch) truffles

12 ounces white chocolate, finely chopped

1 teaspoon instant espresso powder

⅓ cup whipping cream

1½ cups hazelnuts (about 6 ounces), toasted, skinned,
    and finely chopped or ground

1 tablespoon Frangelico (hazelnut liqueur)

Powdered sugar, for dusting hands

Fluted 1-inch paper candy cups (optional)

Step 1 **Place the chocolate** in a large bowl. In a small saucepan over medium heat, dissolve the espresso powder in the cream and bring to a boil. Pour the cream mixture over the chocolate and stir gently with a flexible spatula until the chocolate is melted and smooth. (If the chocolate does not melt completely, place the bowl over a pan of hot water and stir until smooth.) Stir in ½ cup of the hazelnuts and the Frangelico. Cover with plastic wrap and refrigerate until firm enough to scoop, about 3 hours.

Continued on page 62

{ Mocha-Hazelnut Truffles }

Step 2   **Line a baking sheet** with waxed paper. Scoop out tablespoon-size portions of the chocolate mixture; place them on the waxed paper. If the mixture is too firm to scoop, let it stand at room temperature for about 30 minutes to soften.

Step 3   **Place the remaining 1 cup** of hazelnuts on a plate. Dust your hands lightly with powdered sugar. Shape each scoop into a ball, then roll it in the nuts to coat. Place each truffle in a paper candy cup, if desired. Refrigerate the truffles between sheets of waxed paper in an airtight container for up to 1 week.

Chocolate-Dipped Marshmallow Peeps Pops

Who doesn't secretly love marshmallow Peeps bunnies? A layer of good dark chocolate over their crunchy sugar coating transforms this cult favorite into a gourmet candy with a sense of humor. I usually pipe white chocolate dots over the dark chocolate to re-create their signature faces. Once the chocolate has set, you can place a small, clear cellophane treat bag over the bunny and tie a ribbon around the stick. ✎ **Makes:** 24 pops

12 ounces bittersweet or semisweet chocolate, chopped

24 marshmallow Peeps bunnies, separated

24 lollipop sticks (available at candy-supply stores)

1 ounce white chocolate (optional, for eyes)

24 clear cellophane treat bags (optional)

Step 1   **Line a baking sheet** with waxed paper. Melt the chocolate in a bowl set over a pan of hot water (see Melting Chocolate, page 12), stirring frequently until melted and smooth. Remove from the heat.

Step 2   **Insert a stick** into the bottom of each bunny, about halfway up, and dip each one into the chocolate, turning to coat completely. Hold the bunny over the bowl and use a knife to scrape excess chocolate off the back and bottom of the bunny.

Step 3   **Place on the waxed paper face up,** and repeat with the remaining bunnies. If you want to decorate them with faces or other white chocolate accents, melt the white chocolate over hot water and spoon it into a small plastic bag or a pastry bag. Snip off the corner or tip of the bag and pipe dots for eyes. Refrigerate until the chocolate is set, about 1 hour.

Step 4   **Place the pops** in cellophane bags, if desired, and refrigerate in an airtight container for up to 1 week.

Chocolate-Covered Graham Crackers

A few of these graham crackers and a glass of milk are the perfect after-school snack (an important meal for students and non-students alike!). I hold each graham cracker by its edge over the bowl and use a pastry brush to coat the sides and edges with melted chocolate. You'll get a little chocolate on your fingers, but that seems a small price to pay for these satisfying treats. ✐ Makes: 24 crackers

12 whole graham crackers

12 ounces bittersweet or semisweet chocolate, chopped

Step 1   Line 2 baking sheets with waxed paper. Break each cracker in half along its perforation so that you have 24 squares.

Step 2   Melt the chocolate in a bowl set over a pan of hot water (see Melting Chocolate, page 12), stirring frequently until melted and smooth. Remove from the heat.

Step 3   Using a clean pastry brush, coat each cracker with chocolate, covering all sides. Place on the waxed paper and refrigerate until the chocolate is firm, about 1 hour.

Step 4   Store the crackers between sheets of waxed paper in an airtight container at room temperature for up to 1 day, or in the refrigerator for up to 1 week.

Chocolate-Dipped Sesame Halva

Different parts of the world are known for different confections called "halva." The halva I use in this recipe is the crumbly Middle Eastern candy made with tahini (ground sesame seeds) and sugar or honey, available in bars or slabs in Jewish delicatessens or stores that carry Middle Eastern ingredients. Halva is very rich and very sweet, and it makes a spectacular confection when dipped in chocolate. ✎ *Makes: about ½ pound candy*

8 ounces halva

4 ounces bittersweet or semisweet chocolate, chopped

Fluted 1-inch paper candy cups (optional)

Step 1   **Line a baking sheet** with waxed paper. Cut the halva into ½-inch-thick slices and then cut the slices into 1-inch squares (if it came in a slab; otherwise, just cut the bar into squares).

Step 2   **Melt the chocolate** in a bowl set over a pan of hot water (see Melting Chocolate, page 12), stirring frequently until melted and smooth. Remove from the heat.

Step 3   **Gently dip each piece** of halva about halfway into the chocolate and place it on the waxed paper. Sometimes, I find that I have bought halva that is just too crumbly to dip without breaking; if that happens, arrange the squares on waxed paper and carefully spread the melted chocolate over them with a spoon.

Step 4   **Refrigerate until the chocolate is set,** about 30 minutes. Place in paper candy cups, if desired, and store between sheets of waxed paper in an airtight container at room temperature for up to 1 day, or in the refrigerator for up to 1 week.

Chocolate-Dipped Fresh Fruit

The best fresh fruits for dipping are whole with a thin, edible skin and no pit, like strawberries and figs. Sliced fruit is too wet for the chocolate to adhere. Use room-temperature fruit that has been rinsed and patted completely dry. If you want to cover fruit in more than one kind of chocolate (such as strawberries dipped in dark chocolate and then drizzled or partly dipped in white chocolate), let the first chocolate harden in the refrigerator, then apply the second. ✍ **Makes:** 1 pound dipped fruit

6 ounces bittersweet or semisweet chocolate, chopped
1 pound fresh strawberries or figs
2 ounces white chocolate, melted (optional)

Step 1   **Line a baking sheet** with waxed paper. Melt the dark chocolate in a bowl set over a pan of hot water (see Melting Chocolate, page 12), stirring frequently until melted and smooth. Remove from the heat.

Step 2   **Hold each piece of fruit** by the stem end and dip the fruit about three-fourths of the way into the chocolate, shaking any excess chocolate back into the bowl. Place it on the waxed paper.

Step 3   **Refrigerate until the chocolate is set,** about 1 hour. Drizzle with melted white chocolate, if desired. Cover loosely with plastic wrap and store in the refrigerator for up to 1 day.

Chocolate-Dipped Dried Fruit

Dipping dried or candied fruit in chocolate is so simple, but the end result is always impressive. For the most attractive presentation, choose large pieces of dried fruit, such as pear, nectarine, or apricot halves, or dried figs that look moist and intact. Candied pineapple rings, banana chips, papaya spears, or coins of candied ginger are other nice alternatives for dipping. ✎ Makes: about 1 pound dipped fruit

12 ounces bittersweet or semisweet chocolate, chopped

8 ounces dried fruit such as figs, pears, or apricots

Fluted 2- to 3-inch paper candy cups (optional)

Step 1 **Line a baking sheet with waxed paper.** Melt the chocolate in a bowl set over a pan of hot water (see Melting Chocolate, page 12), stirring frequently until melted and smooth. Remove from the heat.

Step 2 **Dip each piece of fruit** about halfway into the chocolate, gently shaking any excess chocolate back into the bowl. Place the fruit on the waxed paper.

Step 3 **Refrigerate until the chocolate is set,** about 1 hour. Place the fruit in paper candy cups, if desired, and store between sheets of waxed paper in an airtight container at room temperature for up to 1 day, or in the refrigerator for up to 1 week.

Chocolate-Dipped Candied Citrus Peel

A little bag of homemade candied citrus peels dipped in chocolate is a beautiful gift, and it's also a nice treat for yourself. ❧ *Makes: about 1 cup chocolate-dipped peels*

8 ounces bittersweet or white chocolate, chopped
1 cup Candied Citrus Peel (page 81)

Step 1   **Line a baking sheet with waxed paper.** Melt the chocolate in a bowl set over a pan of hot water (see Melting Chocolate, page 12), stirring frequently until melted and smooth. Remove from the heat.

Step 2   **Dip the peels** about halfway into the chocolate, shaking any excess chocolate back into the bowl. Place the peels on the waxed paper.

Step 3   **Refrigerate until firm,** about 1 hour. Store in an airtight container in the refrigerator for up to 1 week.

Bonbons and Other Sweetmeats

In this chapter you'll find sweet treats without which any candy collection would be incomplete, from irresistible Toffee Popcorn with Cashews (page 86) to simple and delicious Marzipan-Filled Dates (page 89). A few of these recipes require a little extra time or technique, but I've included them because they are candies that I love, and I think the stunning results are well worth the effort. Imagine passing a plate of Honey-Almond Nougat (page 78), Milk Chocolate Praline (page 82), and lavender-scented Blueberry-Pear Gelées (page 90) after a Provençal-themed dinner. Or making a batch of meltingly creamy Striped Butter Mints (page 85) for a friend's wedding or baby shower. All of the sweets in this chapter make great gifts. There is nothing quite like the gift of homemade caramels, either golden Vanilla–Sea Salt Caramels (page 74) or creamy Butterscotch Caramels (page 77). And I can speak for the baker in your life when I say that a jar of homemade Vanilla Sugar (page 93) would make a unique and welcome present.

✑ Vanilla–Sea Salt Caramels ✑

French caramels are often flavored with sea salt, which cuts the richness and sweetness nicely. An inexpensive square disposable aluminum pan, the kind you can buy in the supermarket, is perfect for making this recipe because you can just bend the sides to release the caramel. Because the pans are fairly flimsy, place a baking sheet underneath for stability when moving the hot caramel.

Waxed paper and white or brown cooking parchment make great wrappers for these caramels. Cut the paper into 4-inch squares (you can measure the first few and then just eyeball the rest). Wrap two sides around each square, as if you were wrapping a present, and then twist the ends closed. ✑ Makes: about 80 caramels

> ¾ cup (1 ½ sticks) unsalted butter, plus more for pan
>
> 2 ¼ cups sugar
>
> 1 cup light corn syrup
>
> 1 cup whipping cream
>
> ½ cup water
>
> 2 ¼ teaspoons sea salt
>
> ½ vanilla bean, split lengthwise and seeds scraped out,
>   or 1 tablespoon vanilla extract

Step 1 : **Generously butter the sides** and bottom of an 8-inch square disposable aluminum cake pan. Place the pan on a baking sheet for stability.

Continued on page 76

{ Vanilla-Sea Salt Caramels }

Step 2

In a large pot over medium-low heat, stir together the sugar, corn syrup, cream, ¾ cup butter, water, salt, and vanilla bean and seeds (if using vanilla extract, don't add yet) until the sugar is dissolved and the butter is melted. Increase the heat and boil, stirring occasionally with a heatproof spatula or a wooden spoon, until the mixture turns a golden brown and measures about 250°F on a candy thermometer, 18 to 25 minutes. Remove from the heat and carefully (the mixture will bubble up) stir in the vanilla extract, if using.

Step 3

Immediately pour the caramel into the prepared pan. Let stand at room temperature until the top is set, about 20 minutes, then refrigerate (with baking sheet underneath) until firm enough to cut, about 2½ hours.

Step 4

Bend back the sides of the pan and invert to release the caramel on to a cutting board. Use a sharp knife to cut the caramel into 1-inch squares. Wrap each piece and store them in an airtight container in the refrigerator for up to 2 weeks. The caramels will taste best if you give them a few minutes at room temperature before eating.

✎ Butterscotch Caramels ✎

You can control the final texture of these caramels by how long you cook them. Cook them to 245°F (soft-ball stage) on your candy thermometer and they will be soft and chewy at room temperature. If you like them firmer, take them to 250°F. S Makes: about 80 caramels

¾ cup (1 ½ sticks) unsalted butter, plus more for pan

2 ¼ cups packed dark brown sugar

1 cup light corn syrup

1 cup whipping cream

½ cup water

1 tablespoon lemon juice

1 teaspoon salt

1 tablespoon vanilla extract

Step 1
Generously butter the sides and bottom of an 8-inch square disposable aluminum cake pan. Place the pan on a baking sheet for stability

Step 2
In a large pot over medium-low heat, stir together the sugar, corn syrup, cream, ¾ cup butter, the water, the lemon juice, and salt until the sugar is dissolved and the butter is melted. Increase the heat and boil, stirring occasionally with a wooden spoon or a heatproof spatula, until the mixture is golden brown and measures 245° to 250°F on a candy thermometer, 10 to 15 minutes. Remove from the heat and carefully (the mixture will bubble up) stir in the vanilla extract.

Step 3
Immediately pour the caramel into the prepared pan. Let stand at room temperature until top is set, about 20 minutes, then refrigerate (with baking sheet underneath) until firm enough to cut, about 2½ hours.

Step 4
Bend back the sides of the pan and invert to release the caramel onto a cutting board. Use a sharp knife to cut the caramel into 1-inch squares. Wrap each piece and store them in an airtight container in the refrigerator for up to 2 weeks. The caramels will taste best if you bring them to room temperature before eating.

✐ Honey-Almond Nougat ✐

This recipe makes a chewy nougat that is somewhere between the Provençal soft nougat (*tendre*) and hard nougat (*dur*). You can substitute hazelnuts or pistachios for some of the almonds, if you like.

You'll need a heavy-duty stand mixer, a candy thermometer, and an 8-inch square disposable aluminum cake pan for this recipe, as well as a sturdy knife for cutting the nougat. Edible wafer paper gives the candy an attractive, finished look. It is available at candy-making supply stores; you might need to trim it or use more than one piece to make an 8-inch square. Or you can omit the wafer paper and use one piece of waxed paper instead. ✐ Makes: about 80 pieces

Canola or flavorless vegetable oil for pan

2 to 4 sheets edible wafer paper or one 8-inch square sheet of waxed paper

2 cups plus 3 tablespoons sugar, divided

¾ cup honey

½ cup water

2 egg whites, at room temperature

1 teaspoon vanilla extract

2 cups whole unsalted almonds (about 11 ounces), lightly toasted

Step 1 : **Lightly oil the sides** of an 8-inch disposable aluminum square cake pan and line the bottom with a single layer of wafer paper. Set aside enough wafer paper to be placed on top of the candy. (If you don't have wafer paper, oil the bottom of the pan as well as the sides, and brush one side of an 8-inch square sheet of waxed paper generously with oil; set waxed paper aside.)

Continued on page 80

{ Honey-Almond Nougat }

Step 2 In a small saucepan that you can lift comfortably with one hand, stir together 2 cups of the sugar, the honey, and water over low heat until the sugar is dissolved. Increase the heat and boil, without stirring, until the mixture measures 320°F on a candy thermometer.

Step 3 Meanwhile, in the bowl of a stand mixer fitted with the whisk attachment, whip the egg whites until frothy. With the mixer running, gradually add the remaining 3 tablespoons of sugar and continue to whip to stiff peaks, 1 to 2 minutes. Turn off the mixer until the sugar mixture is ready.

Step 4 When the sugar mixture reaches 320°F, turn the mixer to high speed and very carefully pour the hot sugar mixture into the whipping egg whites in a slow, steady stream. Continue to whip at high speed until the mixture cools and thickens and becomes almost too stiff to whip, about 10 minutes. Stop the mixer once or twice to scrape down the sides of the bowl. The mixture will start out looking wet and glossy, but as it cools and stiffens, the surface will take on a dull, matte appearance. Add the vanilla and whip for 1 minute.

Step 5 Quickly fold in the almonds and scrape the nougat into the prepared pan. Spread out the candy (it will be very stiff and sticky) with an oiled spatula, and top with another layer of wafer or waxed paper (oiled side down). Flatten the surface by pressing firmly with your hands or a clean spatula. Let the candy stand at room temperature for 8 hours or overnight.

Step 6 Bend back the edges of the pan to loosen the nougat. Remove the waxed paper, if used (leave the edible paper in place), and turn the candy out onto a cutting board. Use a sharp, sturdy knife to cut the nougat into 1-inch squares. Store between sheets of waxed paper in an airtight container at room temperature for up to 1 week.

✒ Candied Citrus Peel ✒

The peels of navel oranges, Meyer lemons, and ruby grapefruit make delicious candy. Candying peels is easier than you think, especially in small batches. You can chop the candied peel and use it in holiday breads, cakes, and shortbread cookies, or dip the peels in chocolate (see page 70). ✒ Makes about 8 ounces candied peels

5 medium oranges, 6 lemons, or 4 grapefruits

2 cups sugar, divided

1½ cup water

Step 1 **Wash the fruit thoroughly.** To remove the peels without tearing, slice off the stem end of the fruit, then make vertical cuts about 1 inch apart through the peel. Carefully peel off the scored sections of rind. With a sharp paring knife, trim away as much of the white pith from the peels as you can. Cut the peels lengthwise into 1/4-inch-wide strips.

Step 2 **In a small pan, cover the peels with water.** Bring to a simmer and cook for 20 minutes. Drain.

Step 3 **In the same pan,** stir together 1 1/2 cups of the sugar and the water over medium-low heat until the sugar is dissolved. Add the peels and simmer gently, stirring occasionally, until soft and translucent, about 40 minutes.

Step 4 **Place a cooling rack** over a baking sheet and use a slotted spoon or tongs to transfer the peels to the rack. Let them stand until almost dry, about 1 hour.

Step 5 **Line a baking sheet** with waxed paper. Place the remaining 1/2 cup of the sugar in a bowl. Roll the peels in the sugar to coat, shaking off any excess. Place the peels on the waxed paper and let them dry completely, about 4 hours. Store in an airtight container at room temperature for up to 1 month.

Milk Chocolate Praline

Milk chocolate filled with crunchy hazelnut praline is a French confection that is often used as an ingredient in desserts and pastries, but it is a delicious candy in its own right. To crush the praline neatly, seal pieces in a plastic bag and crush with a rolling pin or mallet. This recipe makes about 3 cups crushed praline, and you will only need 2 cups. Store the remaining praline airtight at room temperature, and use it to sprinkle over ice cream, in between cake layers, or mix it into shortbread or chocolate chip cookie dough. ✐ Makes: about 80 (1-inch) squares

Butter for the pan

1 ½ cups sugar

½ cup water

1 tablespoon light corn syrup

1 ½ cups almonds or hazelnuts (about 8 ounces),
   lightly toasted and finely chopped

¼ teaspoon salt

12 ounces milk chocolate, chopped

4 ounces bittersweet chocolate, chopped

Fluted 1-inch paper candy cups (optional)

Step 1	**Lightly butter** a 10-by-15-inch jelly-roll pan.
Step 2	**Combine the sugar,** water, and corn syrup in a small saucepan. Stir over medium heat until the sugar is dissolved, about 5 minutes. Increase the heat to high and boil without stirring until golden brown (335° to 340°F on a candy thermometer), 10 to 15 minutes. When the sugar begins to brown around the edges of the pan, swirl it gently so that it caramelizes evenly.
Step 3	**Remove from the heat.** Quickly and carefully stir in the nuts and salt and spread the mixture onto the prepared pan. Let it stand at room temperature until cool, about 1 hour. Break into pieces and chop or crush the praline very finely.
Step 4	**Line an 8-inch square baking pan** with aluminum foil (if you use a disposable aluminum pan, there's no need to line it). Melt the chocolates together in a bowl set over a pan of hot water (see Melting Chocolate, page 12), stirring occasionally until smooth. Stir in 2 cups of the crushed praline and spread the mixture in the prepared pan. Refrigerate until firm enough to cut, about 1 hour.
Step 5	**Invert the pan** to remove the candy and cut it into 1-inch squares with a sharp, sturdy knife. Place the squares in paper candy cups, if desired. Store in an airtight container at room temperature for up to 2 days, or in the refrigerator for up to 1 week.

Striped Butter Mints

If your only experience with butter mints has been those little rock-hard pastel pillows at bridal showers, you will be amazed by these delicate, creamy candies. Red and green stripes make them great for Christmas, but use other colors to make them appropriate for different occasions.

Gel food coloring and peppermint oil are available at stores that sell candy-making supplies. You can substitute regular food coloring and peppermint extract, but neither the flavor nor the color will be quite as intense. Makes: about 1 pound mints

4¼ to 4½ cups powdered sugar, plus more for dusting
¼ cup (½ stick) unsalted butter, at room temperature
¼ cup whipping cream
⅛ teaspoon peppermint oil
Gel food coloring

Step 1
With a mixer on low speed, beat together the sugar, the butter, cream, and peppermint oil until well blended. The mixture will be stiff; when it becomes too stiff for the mixer, turn it out onto a surface lightly sprinkled with powdered sugar and knead by hand, working in more powdered sugar as necessary, until the mixture is soft and smooth but not sticky.

Step 2
Divide the mixture into 8 pieces. Working with 1 piece at a time (cover the remaining pieces with plastic wrap while you work, to prevent them from drying out), add a few drops of red and green (or other) food coloring to different spots, and work the piece gently in your hands until the color is distributed in irregular streaks (to tint the mints a solid color, just mix the food coloring completely in until no streaks remain). On a surface dusted with powdered sugar, roll each piece into a rope about 10 inches long and ¼ inch thick. With a sharp knife, cut the rope into ¼-inch squares. Place the mints on a waxed paper–lined baking sheet.

Step 3
Cover the mints loosely with a second sheet of waxed paper and let them stand at room temperature until dry, about 8 hours. Refrigerate in an airtight container for up to 1 week.

Toffee Popcorn with Cashews

There are many reasons to make this buttery candied popcorn, but you don't really *need* a reason at all. If you don't have an air popper, just be sure to use popcorn without butter or additional seasonings. ∾ Makes: about 9 cups popcorn

8 cups air-popped popcorn

½ cup (1 stick) unsalted butter, cut into chunks, plus more for pan

1 cup unsalted cashews (about 6 ounces), lightly toasted

1 ¼ cups sugar

¼ cup water

2 tablespoons corn syrup

½ teaspoon salt

1 teaspoon vanilla extract

Step 1 | **Place the popcorn** and cashews in a large bowl. Lightly butter a 10-by-15-inch jelly-roll pan.

Step 2 | **In a medium saucepan** over medium-low heat, stir together the sugar, ½ cup butter, the water, corn syrup, and salt until the sugar is dissolved and the butter is melted. Increase the heat and bring to a simmer. Cook, stirring occasionally with a heatproof spatula or a wooden spoon, until the mixture turns a deep golden brown (290° to 300°F on a candy thermometer), 5 to 8 minutes. Remove from the heat and carefully (the mixture will bubble up) stir in the vanilla. Immediately pour over the popcorn and cashews and mix gently to coat with a spatula or spoon.

Step 3 | **Scrape the mixture** out onto the prepared pan, spreading the popcorn out flat with an oiled spatula. Let it cool at room temperature until hard, about 30 minutes. Break apart and transfer to an airtight container. Store at room temperature for up to 1 week.

✍ Marzipan-Filled Dates ✍

Soft, sweet California Medjool dates are at their peak during the winter months, and this quick snack or dessert is a great way to take advantage of them. This recipe is for one pound of dates, but it's easy to make them in any quantity. Marzipan is sweeter and has a more pronounced bitter-almond flavor than almond paste, but both are delicious with the dates. ✍ Makes: 1 pound stuffed dates

1 pound Medjool dates
6 ounces marzipan or almond paste

Step 1   Cut the dates almost in half lengthwise and remove the pits without completely separating the two halves, if you can. Break off ½-inch chunks of marzipan or almond paste (a little smaller than 1 teaspoon) and shape them into an oval with your fingers. Place the marzipan in the center of each date and press the halves together, leaving a little of the marzipan showing.

Step 2   Refrigerate in an airtight container for up to 1 week.

Blueberry-Pear Gelées

These beautiful candies, which are also called *pâtes de fruits*, are delicious, sugar-covered squares of concentrated fruit. They have a reputation for being difficult to make, but the only trick is that the fruit mixture needs to be cooked a long time over low heat, until it has cooked down to a thick paste about the consistency of a thick applesauce. Depending on your pan, stove, and the water content of the pears, this might take anywhere from 1¼ hours to 2 hours, so be patient and keep cooking until the mixture looks thick enough that you'll have to spread it smoothly in the pan. Makes: about 60 gelées

2 pounds Bartlett or Anjou pears

1 pound frozen blueberries

4 cups sugar, divided

½ cup water

Two 3-ounce packages Certo liquid pectin

3 tablespoons lemon juice

1 tablespoon finely ground culinary lavender

Fluted 1-inch paper candy cups (optional)

Step 1 — Line an 8-inch square pan with foil (or use a disposable aluminum cake pan).

Step 2 — Rinse the pears thoroughly. Quarter, core, and cut them into chunks (don't peel; the peel has additional pectin, which helps the gelées set). In a medium saucepan over medium heat, stir together the pears, blueberries, 2 cups of the sugar, and the water and simmer gently until the pears are very soft, about 20 minutes. Let the mixture cool slightly, then puree it in batches in a blender or food processor until smooth.

Continued on page 92

{ Blueberry-Pear Gelées }

Step 3

Return the puree to the saucepan and add the pectin, lemon juice, lavender, and 1 cup of the sugar. Bring to a low simmer and cook, stirring frequently, especially as it reduces, until the mixture is quite thick, 1 hour to 1 hour and 15 minutes. It should be thick enough that when you run a spatula across the bottom of the pan, you can see the bottom of the pan for a moment before the mixture covers it again. Scrape the mixture into the prepared pan and smooth the surface with a spatula. Let it cool at room temperature for 1 hour, then cover the surface with plastic wrap and refrigerate for at least 2 more hours, or up to 2 weeks.

Step 4

Just before serving, place the remaining 1 cup of sugar on a plate. Remove the candy by inverting the pan onto a cutting board. Trim the edges and cut the candy into ¾-inch squares. Roll the squares in sugar to coat. Place them in paper candy cups, if desired.

❧ Vanilla Sugar ❧

Bakers will appreciate this perfumed sugar as a nice addition to cakes or egg breads, or sprinkled on the tops of muffins or scones before baking. It is also nice on the outside of Blueberry-Pear Gelées (page 90) or Candied Citrus Peel (page 81). I like to fill a pretty glass jar with this sugar and give it as a gift along with some good black tea. Choose a plump, moist-looking vanilla bean. ❧ Makes: 1½ cups vanilla sugar

1 vanilla bean

1½ cups sugar

Step 1 — **Split the bean lengthwise.** In the bowl of a food processor fitted with the steel blade, scrape the seeds from the vanilla bean into the sugar. Pulse until well distributed. Spoon the sugar into a pint-size jar and tuck in the empty vanilla bean pod. The sugar will keep indefinitely at room temperature.

Index

Table of Equivalents

The exact equivalents in the following tables have been rounded for convenience.

Liquid/Dry Measurements

U.S.	METRIC
¼ teaspoon	1.25 milliliters
½ teaspoon	2.5 milliliters
1 teaspoon	5 milliliters
1 tablespoon (3 teaspoons)	15 milliliters
1 fluid ounce (2 tablespoons)	30 milliliters
¼ cup	60 milliliters
⅓ cup	80 milliliters
½ cup	120 milliliters
1 cup	240 milliliters
1 pint (2 cups)	480 milliliters
1 quart (4 cups, 32 ounces)	960 milliliters
1 gallon (4 quarts)	3.84 liters
1 ounce (by weight)	28 grams
1 pound	448 grams
2.2 pounds	1 kilogram

Lengths

U.S.	METRIC
⅛ inch	3 millimeters
¼ inch	6 millimeters
½ inch	12 millimeters
1 inch	2.5 centimeters

Oven Temperature

FAHRENHEIT	CELSIUS	GAS
250	120	½
275	140	1
300	150	2
325	160	3
350	180	4
375	190	5
400	200	6
425	220	7
450	230	8
475	240	9
500	260	10